THE FORENSIC PSYCHOLOGY OF FALSE ALLEGATIONS

CONNOR WHITELEY

No part of this book may be reproduced in any form or by any electronic or mechanical means. Including information storage, and retrieval systems, without written permission from the author except for the use of brief quotations in a book review.

This book is NOT legal, professional, medical, financial or any type of official advice.

Any questions about the book, rights licensing, or to contact the author, please email connorwhiteley@connorwhiteley.net

Copyright © 2024 CONNOR WHITELEY

All rights reserved.

DEDICATION
Thank you to all my readers without you I couldn't do what I love.

INTRODUCTION

Whenever a crime happens, a victim has to gather up the courage to go to a police station or dial 999 or 911 and they have to report the crime by making an allegation that a crime has occurred in the first place.

Sometimes these allegations are true, other times they are not.

In this fascinating brand-new book by international bestseller Connor Whiteley, we're going to be exploring why on Earth someone would make a false allegation, claiming that a crime has happened to them when it has not.

This great book focuses on the legality, psychological factors and a wide range of additional factors that play a role in someone deciding and making a false allegation that can ultimately destroy lives, take people away from their loved ones and cause people a lot of pain.

<u>Trigger Warning</u>

The main focus of this book is false allegations of rape, sexual assault and child sexual abuse. Whilst this book does NOT go into any cases in depth or in any graphic detail, I want to mention this upfront so you can get prepared to read, learn and deepen your understanding of these topics.

In addition, the entire point of this book is definitely not to imply that all allegations involving these crimes are false. This is NOT the message of the book at all and time after time in this book, we are reminded about the true number of how many allegations are real.

Why Buy This Book?

There are a lot of myths and misconceptions about false allegations. Therefore, this great, easy-to-understand book helps readers to understand and deepen their knowledge about a topic that is rarely spoken about or taught in wider society.

As a result, by the end of this book, you will know:

- What are the problems with false allegations?
- How do thinking and memory biases impact false allegations?
- How do mental health conditions and personality factors impact false allegations?
- What is the Recovered Memory/ False Memory debate and why is this important?
- And so much more

If you're interested in forensic psychology, cognitive psychology and social psychology then you are going to be in for a real treat, as you learn about a great area of psychology.

In addition, like always, this book is written in my normal engaging and conversational tone that helps to bring the topic alive and make it interesting. This is nothing like the dull boring university textbooks we all enjoyed at university, besides from its fact-based nature.

Who Am I?

Personally, I always love to know who the author is of the nonfiction I read so I know the information is coming from a good source. In case you're like me, I'm Connor Whiteley, the internationally bestselling author of over 40 psychology books.

In addition, I am the host of *The Psychology World Podcast,* a weekly show exploring a new psychology topic each week and delivering the latest psychology news. Available on all major podcast apps and YouTube.

Finally, I am a psychology graduate studying a Clinical Psychology Masters at the University of Kent, England.

So now we know more about each other, let's dive into the great topic of the forensic psychology of false allegations.

WHAT ARE FALSE ALLEGATIONS?

Kicking off the book and the forensic psychology of false allegations, we need to understand what these actually are before we can explore the psychology behind them. This is even more important when we consider that false allegations aren't really anything to do with psychology, so why are forensic psychologists still interested?

That's what we'll explore in this first chapter.

Therefore, false allegations are all about miscarriages of justice. Since if a false allegation is made then this does have the potential to lead to a criminal investigation, court and maybe even a conviction based on a false allegation.

As you'll see throughout the book it is rarely that simple but it can happen.

As a result, a miscarriage of justice is rather difficult to define, because the easiest definition we'll be using for this book is *when an innocent person gets convicted for a crime they didn't commit.*

On the surface that sounds like a perfect definition, and in theory it certainly is, but if we want to apply that definition to the real world then we experience one problem after another. Since whilst a miscarriage of justice is when a court of appeal overturns a conviction (Naugton, 2005). This is important to know because miscarriages of justice are the results of false allegations. But an overturned conviction doesn't always mean the person was believed to be innocent.

A conviction could be overturned due to police mishandling the evidence, a witnessed lied or another of a whole range of factors.

Therefore, as you can start to notice, this is more of a legal question than a psychological question but I promise you the link between psychology and miscarriages of justice is coming up soon.

On the whole, it is very, very difficult to get a true rate of fake allegations as that depends on the definition being used.

For example, a researcher or another person couldn't use all non-guilty verdicts to imply that a false allegation against the accused has happened. When in reality all a non-guilty verdict means is that it was beyond reasonable doubt that the accused did not commit the crime.

Another example that makes the true rate hard to know about is "unfounded claims" were no supporting evidence is found. These are different to false allegations because in false allegations no crime actually happened, but in unfounded claims, an offense could have happened but there is no evidence of it ever happening.

This is certainly a reason why I like legal stuff because it is so complex but extremely interesting at the same time.

In addition, recanted accusations aren't evidence that no offense occurred because different people recant their statements for different reasons. Including the reconciliation between partners.

As well as this is before we consider the clear difference between false allegations and false convictions. It is these differences that make a true rate of false allegations next to impossible to know.

So are false allegations a problem and why should we care?

<u>Why We Need To Care About False Allegations?</u>

Of all the different types of false allegations, child sexual abuse is one of the most important areas and this is the area where the most false allegations are made. As well as this will be the focus of the book because it is such a heart-breaking, important and unfortunate area of human behaviour.

For example, Poole and Lindsay (1998) found that false allegations make up 5%-8% of all child sexual abuse cases and this only includes those cases that involved intentional false allegations.

Therefore, because this is only focusing on malicious motives behind the false allegation, this covers up a much, much greater number of child sexual abuse cases.

Whereas other studies propose that false allegations make up between 23%-35% of all cases (Howitt, 1992). And I have to admit that yes, at first this might sound very high but if we convert these percentages into real numbers, the numbers get scary.

If a police force had, let's say, 1,000 sexual abuse cases. According to these numbers 230- 350 of these cases would be false, allegations. That would mean a hell of a lot of time, police resources and emotional distress would be wasted. Just because someone decided to make a false allegation.

And then my personal pet hate is that those 350 fake cases would cast doubt on the millions of real ones.

In addition, it is important to remember that in this book, we will talk about a lot of numbers. But it is critical that we remember that behind each of these numbers there is a ton of trauma, distress and more negative experiences for the child and family.

This is even more important when we consider that the consequences of false allegations include a child being removed from home, the father being made to live away from home and imprisoned and even well-intentioned false allegations can take a toll on family life (Howitt, 1992). As well as false denials by victims of abuse can equally as damaging. (Lyon, 1995).

Overall, this is why it is of immense interest to psychologists, because someone making a false allegation, that is a human behaviour. Also, the consequences, the emotional trauma and the pain that the child and family experience, they are all human behaviours and considering psychologists are experts on the matter. That is why we are so critical to understanding why this awful facet of human behaviour happens in the first place.

But let's explore more about why are false allegations so problematic for psychologists?

PROBLEMS OF FALSE ALLEGATIONS

There are a ton of problems that psychology researchers face when it comes to false allegations that we'll look at in the course of the book, but one of the most immediate problems is that the police are rather bad at keeping records.

Since don't get me wrong, I know that the police are very underfunded, they are a service-based organisation that focuses on serving the community, but it would be nice if their crime reporting was a bit easier for psychology researchers to use.

For example, police crime reports are obvious sources of information for us about false allegations, but they are very problematic. Since the International Association Of Chiefs Of Police (2005) proposed that a case would count as a false allegation if there is real evidence that a crime never happened.

That isn't a bad definition to be honest and it is true for the most part. If a person makes an allegation about a crime that never happened, then that is a false allegation.

The problem is that sloppy and errored police work only increases this number, and this can be best seen in rape cases. Due to the disgusting nature of these cases, it can be very hard to get proper evidence on rapists and sometimes police don't really bother investigating to some extent.

As a result of these cases that find no real evidence of a crime happening, the USA uses the term "unfounded" in police reports to mean this is a fake allegation or without foundation after they've conducted a proper investigation. Whereas the UK uses the much simpler term "No Crime".

Although, as good as those words are, they aren't actually synonymous with false allegations as they include other situations.

For instance, if a woman is at a party and she claims to be raped but she doesn't know if sexual penetration has happened. Then she could easily fall into this No Crime category because the most basic legal requirement for something to be classed as rape is sexual penetration. Therefore, it is unknown if this most basic requirement has been met.

But that isn't the same as a false allegation because she isn't saying a crime didn't happen, she's simply saying she's not 100% sure if she was penetrated.

Furthermore, this is even worse because research has repeatedly shown that the police don't follow their own rules when classifying crimes. For example, the official rules for ruling cases as Unfounded or No Crime are a lot stricter and there are more cases in these categories than strict interpretation would ever allow.

One such study is Lisak, Gardinier, Nick and Cote (2010) who looked at examples of when the police misclassified cases wrongly. Some of the cases that were wrongly put into Unfounded or No Crime categories included when the victim for whatever reason is uncooperative with cops, when the victim delays the reporting, when the victim was intoxicated, police failed to obtain sufficient evidence to prosecute as well as cases involving where victims directly lies or offers inconsistent accounts.

As you can see none of those cases imply that a crime didn't happen. For instance, going back to the woman at the party example and she was raped. If she was drinking and raped, the police might have said a crime didn't happen because the victim was drunk.

Or if the police found good amounts of evidence that a rape happened but not enough that it could go to court, that doesn't mean it was a false allegation because evidence was found. Yet the police still might classify it as such.

It is bad and hopefully that might change in the future.

Another research example comes from Lisak et al (2010) who studied sexual assault reports for a 10-year period and categorised them into 3 categories to avoid solely relying on original investigations. This would help to avoid the reports that weren't actually false allegations.

Therefore, the researchers found that there were 6% of false reports in the sample. This judgement was based on there being no evidence of a crime. Also, 35% of the sample was put into the Case Proceeded pile because the police or investigators past the case onto prosecution. Finally, the last category made up 45% of the sample where the Cases Didn't Proceed to prosecution or another type of action. This could have been down to a lack of evidence, the perpetrator couldn't be identified, victim withdrew complaint and the allegations weren't a crime in legal terms.

However, there was insufficient information to categorise about 14% of cases, meaning that the report and file contained very little information.

Yet when the researchers coded the sample, there was an inter-range agreement of 95% for the false report category so this means there are extremely high accuracy. Making the researchers confident that the false allegation rate was 6% for the sample. As well as this is well within the range as found by other researchers.

Then the only real negative about this study is that the 6% figure is for sustained false allegations. Therefore, it is perfectly possible that other false allegations were subsumed into other categories.

Overall, this is a good study to look at because it helps us to understand the "real" false allegation rate when we control for factors like sloppy and bad police work. This is a good basis to build upon for our later chapters when we start to look at the psychology behind why people make false allegations.

British Home Office Research

The third research example I want to look at comes from Kelly, Lovett and Regan (2005) and their study of false allegations that was commissioned by the British Home Office. The researchers used a large number of rape cases from a 15-year period and the sample used a wide range of sources that the researchers draw on. For example, any interviews, medical reports, forensic reports and more that were connected to the rape.

The results demonstrated that the police used the "No Crime" category as a dustbin category for different things. Meaning according to the police 8% of these rape cases across the 15 years were false allegations, but sometimes this was merely down to police scepticism instead of real police work. As there were cases where the police didn't have evidence that No Crime had occurred.

Therefore, the researchers reanalysed all the cases according to Home Office rules (so the rules that the police are *meant* to follow in the real world but don't), and the researchers found that if these rules were followed then the false allegation rate could have been 3%.

The Role of Public Opinion In False Allegations

As much as I love forensic psychology and laypeople, I have to admit that the role that public opinion plays in the Criminal Justice System is beyond annoying and I flat out hate it. My little soap box is that we have mountains beyond mountains of good research showing that if we want to decrease reoffending and make prison "work". Then you have to rehabilitate criminals, help them develop new skills and help them build a life for themselves.

That is proven time and time again in good research.

However, the general public thinks that is a lie and criminals need to be punished, no politician or government invests in rehabilitation programmes. So criminals go to jail, do their time, come out the exact same as before and commit another crime. Costing taxpayers more and more compared to breaking the cycle of criminal activity through rehabilitation.

Anyway that is just my little soapbox.

The reason why I'm talking about this is because public opinion and the opinion of other legal professionals really impact false allegations. Due to these really low rates contrast with what staff working in the Criminal Justice System believe.

As supported by Saunders (2012) who interviewed UK Crown Prosecutors and police officers and their results showed they appear to think false allegation rates are higher.

Leading researchers to argue that this reflects biases by the Criminal Justice System against victims of rape, but then again researchers themselves do need to clarify how they know offenses did or didn't happen.

As a result, Saunders argues that studies requiring positive evidence of no offense (which are the rules I add) give low estimates. Typically between 2% to 11%.

This could be the end of the matter but researchers don't systematically investigate false allegations of rape, and instead often scrutinize police "no crime" decision. And I think we can all see this throughout the chapter, these studies before now have been looking at No Crime decisions instead of the rapes themselves.

Moreover, because of the Home Office "no crime" rules, Saunders argues this isn't the same as the false allegation definition. She says this merely shows when a report can be knocked off the total tally for this crime.

And this I think is critical to understand. There is a massive difference between false allegations and just knocking off reports so the real rate of a crime can be lowered. If anyone has ever had an experience or read up on Hate Crimes then this is all too common. A Hate Crime will happen but I always find it shocking when it is actually reported as such because the rates are really low compared to reality.

Also, Saunders interviewed prosecutors and police officers about false allegations and found they tended to believe false allegations were relatively rare but believed fake partial or completely fake statements to be common.

Now that we know the problems with false allegation research, let's start tapping into the psychology behind false allegations, because what are the pathways to making one?

PATHWAYS TO FALSE ALLEGATIONS

Moving onto the more psychology-focused content of the book, in this chapter, we're going to focus on the various ways and reasons why people make false allegations. Also, this chapter is all about setting up different parts of the rest of the book, all whilst being very useful in its own right.

Therefore, from a historical viewpoint, it was presumed that rape victims were always to blame and that sex offences were trivial matters that didn't matter very much. I'm extremely grateful that we have (for the most part) moved beyond this false belief, because this is flat out wrong.

Furthermore, historically, people believed that no women were actually raped and women only "cried rape" so they could get revenge over someone, or they did it for another malicious reason. Historically, people even went as far as to give victims a made-up mental health condition because they said they were raped. Pseudologia phantastia was the phrase used to describe cases of this hypothetical condition where women were apparently in a deluded state that caused them to falsely claim they were raped (Bessmer, 1984).

It is outrageous that rape was regarded with such indifference in the past, but thankfully we have moved past this for the most part. Resulting in the current presumption being that victims are telling the truth. The way it should always be.

This is important to remember because child sexual abuse caseloads are filled with examples of false allegations that are made against parents and others. These false allegations are made because of a range of reasons. For instance, in most cases no physical evidence can be found, and whilst penetrative sex might damage the anus or reproductive organs of a physically immature child. This is only one example of sexual abuse and there are plenty of others. For example, oral sex leaves no traces. As well as some cases can't always be supported by medical evidence.

Another reason can be found in cases where there is little evidence, but there is some evidence coming from interviewing children. This can be a cause of false allegations because unskilled interviewing could lead to fake information from the child. This is a massive section later on in the book.

That's why it is important that the public and professionals that want to protect children everywhere need to make sure they don't overact to something a child has said.

In addition, there are some family circumstances that are conductive of false allegations from children as supported by Lipian, Mills and Brantman (2004). As well as false allegations can experience a sort of contagion effect when other youngsters come forward with reports.

This I think is particularly heartbreaking but we talk about it more in a moment.

Furthermore, when parents are getting divorced, a parent might try and influence an impressionable child somehow to make them give false allegations of abuse against the person they're divorcing.

Equally, even children in non-abusive but still dysfunctional families might make false allegations as a cry for help. This is even more important when we consider that in dysfunctional families, an adolescent could make a false allegation for secondary gains. These secondary gains include getting back at the family or deflecting family outrage at a situation. Like, an unacceptable boyfriend or girlfriend or a teenage pregnancy.

Personally, I think one of the most heartbreaking reasons of all is when false allegations are made if the child who makes the allegation has learnt from past abuse about the sheer power of a revelation so years later make a false allegation to act as a bombshell to try and stop something happening that they didn't want to happen.

<u>Why Are False Allegations So Difficult To</u>

Investigate?

However, I know in the last section of the chapter and the chapter before that I have mentioned that sometimes false allegations are simply down to bad police work, and they really are a good chunk of the time.

However, we have to realise and we cannot afford to overestimate the sheer amount of difficulty facing investigators in these situations. This is even more true when young children are involved, so we'll explore the reasons behind this in later chapters of the book.

One of the main reasons why this is the case is that independent evidence is very hard to get when it comes to abuse, as well as the offender is unlikely to confess. And come on, if you were foul enough to abuse someone, you really wouldn't confess to it because of all the stigma and shame that is thankfully attached to abuse.

As a result, only 30% of offenders fully or partially confess to abuse (Lippert, Cross, Jones and Walsh, 2010) meaning that there's still 70% of offenders that the police have to try to find evidence against.

This isn't an easy job at all.

In addition, this 30% figure is further supported by research findings from polygraph studies too, but in these cases confessions are slightly more likely to happen.

Moreover, there are factors that encourage

confessions of abuse. These include, when a suspect is younger, when the abuse victim is older, when there is a greater amount of evidence, if the abuse case is outside of the family and when there is more evidence.

I don't think any of them are too surprising.

Some other factors that encourage confessions are:

- If a child disclosures the abuse fully.
- Abuse is more severe.
- More victims come forward.
- There is corroborating evidence of the abuse.

Therefore, as you can imagine, as amazing as these factors are and I think every single police officer can support me here, that if we knew factors that would 100% encourage a confession then the life of a police officer would be great.

Yet these factors are extremely hard to come by.

So it shouldn't be too surprising if an offender denies everything said against them.

In terms of next steps for psychologists and police officers, we need psychological research to embrace the full range of motives as well as processes that are involved in producing false allegations.

This is where a useful introspection comes in from O'Donohue and Boven's (2006) because they focus on the complexity of false allegations in their theoretical analysis of sexual harassment allegations. Due to they propose that there are a number of

pathways or factors involved in false allegations. These include:
- Psychosis
- Dementia
- Substance abuse
- Lying
- Biased interviews
- False memories
- Investigative errors

We'll look at a lot of these now and in the next couple of chapters, but we need to remember that most pathways are complex in themselves and this is largely speculative theorising that was extended by Engle and O'Donohue (2012) including a psychological condition conducive for making false allegations of sexual assault. Yet the evidence for each of these pathways is limited at best.

Also, these are basically impossible to look at and test in a research setting. For example, it would be very hard to test how false memories lead to false allegations, because you flat out cannot manipulate a variable and make someone make a false allegation against something.

How These Different Factors Impact False Allegations?

Now we're going to look at some of the pathways and factors that lead to False Allegations in more depth.

Firstly, false allegations can occur when someone

lies for unconscious or conscious secondary gains and this is the typical pathway that's considered when false allegations are suspected. These secondary gains can include attention, trouble and punishing parents.

Secondly, this is something we dedicate a chapter to later on, but fake memories can cause false allegations. Since research shows that fake memories can be created in different situations. As a result, false memories of an event can lead to a false allegation, and if you want to know more about false memories, definitely check out [Cognitive Psychology](#).

Thirdly, intoxication is a factor and plays a role in false allegations. Due to alcohol and other drugs lead to poor information processes so there is a lot of confusion about what did happen and what didn't happen at a particular event. As well as people that are under the influence of any substance cannot give consent in most US states and UK (Sexual Offences Act, 2003) and elsewhere. Meaning that if a person believes they were interfered with during an event then this can lead to a false allegation.

Building upon this point, denial of consent is when a legal issue might not be whether the sexual act happened or not but whether consent was given. Since sexual relationships aren't formal contracts and consent can be non-verbal too. Therefore, this sadly leaves room for mistakes and misunderstandings with some offenders purposefully misunderstanding the intent of their victim.

Personally, I will definitely jump in here and just

say that men and women, please whenever you want to have sex with someone, make sure you give verbal consent. That way things are clear and misunderstandings are hopefully a lot less likely to happen.

In addition, Anti-social Personal Disorder (or Conduct Disorder for adolescence) is a mental health condition that impacts false allegations. Since this is a general pattern of informing (and violating) the rights of others, with the diagnostic characteristics including non-conforming to social norms as well as being remorseless and deceitfulness. Consequently, this could actually increase and encourage false allegations. Since people with the condition are more likely to be perpetrators and report being sexually victimised when compared to other people (Burnman et al., 1988).

Now our fourth-to-last one is really interesting I think because it is something we rarely hear about in psychology, at least in my own experience. Due to delirium is a disturbance of consciousness with cognitive changes that aren't the result of dementia, as well as perceptual disturbances. This is where misinterpretation and illusions can happen because of a range of causes. Like a medical condition and substance abuse. This connects to false allegations because sufferers need to be closely monitored and cared for so this can be misinterpreted as sexual by sufferers experiencing this.

In addition, as much as the term "Borderline

Personality Disorder" is outdated, because it is now thankfully called Complex Emotional Needs. I need to call it that because a lot of people reading this book will still know it as BPD.

As a result, this condition has features including relationship difficulties, impulsivity as well as frequently involves feelings of abandonment. Also, they may experience cognitive disturbances, like disassociation, delusions, hallucinations and extreme feelings of badness. And the interesting thing about this is that a person with Complex Emotional Needs can rapidly change from idealising to devaluing a partner so they might make a false allegation against the partner to punish them for past behaviour.

Now I still find that fascinating because "logically" speaking and as a person who doesn't have that mental health condition, it makes no sense to me. And that is what makes psychology such an interesting topic because it's fun to learn about how others perceive the world.

And there is nothing wrong at all about learning about other people that are different to ourselves.

Penultimately, as some of you who are familiar with psychosis might have guessed, psychotic disorders have a role to play in false allegations too. Since psychotic states are characterised by delusions and hallucinations with a range of common delusions can be experienced. For example, one of my favourite types of delusions because I've used this to start off a Matilda Plum fantasy short story before, is erotomaniac where the person experiencing psychosis strongly believes that someone else is in love with them despite this not being the case at all. These beliefs are irrational and unsubstantiated. Resulting in people with the condition at times being associated with persecutory delusions so these people can believe someone is sexually persecuting them or harming them so that's how a false allegation can be made against someone.

Finally, Histrionic personality disorder is a mental health condition I've never heard of before I started researching this topic. It is a condition involving an excessive and widespread emotionality coupled with attention-seeking behaviour that are the main characteristics of the condition. These people are uncomfortable unless they're the centre of attention when interacting with others when they may be overtly suggestive and seductive. Leading to a false allegation could be stimulating to them because it brings the focus back on them. This is why they misconstrue compliments as sexual pass or physical contact as deliberate.

Therefore, this is what I mean about false allegations aren't always done out of hate or something. They can simply be down to other factors that a person might not have control over.

That is why this topic is so interesting because it seriously isn't as flat and dry as the media and others make out.

However, do false memories really play a role in

false allegations or could these memories be recovered memories of a real past event?

Turn over the page and let's find out.

THE FORENSIC PSYCHOLOGY OF FALSE ALLEGATIONS

WHAT IS THE RECOVERED MEMORY/ FALSE MEMORY DEBATE?

We're definitely moving onto one of the best chapters in the entire book because I have to admit I love this debate. It is fascinating, filled with twists and turns and this is a lot of fun to talk about.

Therefore, to start off the chapter, if you've ever read or done Cognitive Psychology before then you're familiar that human memory isn't a camera or video recorder. It isn't perfect because humans can and do edit, rearrange and create entire memories that never happened.

This is when false memories come in since people without knowing it can recreate or add in memories that never happened at all.

In addition, you probably know that an interview technique can create false allegations through repeated suggestive interviews and leading questions, but the repeated sessions aren't always needed.

As showed by Bernet (1997) when the researcher investigated when an allegation was made by a concerned babysitter after she taped an interview with a child filled with suggestions. In this case, the babysitter gave forced-choice alternatives that shaped in the child's mind they were being molested.

Overall, the paper was looking at how the power of suggestion impacts a person's memory. This is a major focus now for the rest of the book.

Leading to one of the most controversial debates in modern psychology (Ost et al., 2013) and unfortunately this debate gets used in courtrooms in addition to academic journals.

Personally, I say unfortunate because you can probably guess the arguments made in this chapter can be abused by lawyers wanting to defend their clients. It is a shame that psychology debates can be used as a legal defence but I suppose if you can't use debates to make a point for or against someone in court, then what is the point of them?

I am joking by the way.

Anyway, a flavour of the debate can be found in Kristiansen, Felton and Hordested's (1996) who wrote that recovered memory/ false memories are more "closely tied to autocratic misogyny and self-interested than they are social values of science" (page 38).

Mainly because there seems to be plenty of "facts" for any position a particular person wants to defend.

Additionally, whilst there are a lot of factors in the formation of this psychology debate, one of the most significant factors is the allegation made by psychology professor Jennifer Freyd (1996) against her parents (Calof, 1993) for child abuse against her. Leading to the creation of the False Memory Syndrome Foundation.

Due to when the professor was an adult, she was being treated by a psychologist in therapy and this led to the debate about if the psychologist suggested the abuse or helped to recover repressed memories.

Now for something to be officially diagnosed as a Recovered Memory, two important steps have to be fulfilled. First the child would have to deal with this trauma by a state of amnesia then, secondly, get the therapist to reliably help the child or adult client recover them.

The central issue is concerning the therapist and client, because the issues is we simply don't know with 100% empirical certainty that these are recovered memories and not a therapist simply implanting these memories of abuse. And this is an important issue that's being rehearsed in the courtrooms and legal settings everywhere.

Furthermore, MacMartin and Yarney (1998) relate the dispute between who as the expertise on this matter, because the literature on the topic is seen as a battle between academics and clinical practitioners.

Personally, I am so glad I am not an academic nor a clinical psychologist just yet, because my hands are relatively clean here. Yet the support for recovered memories as reliable indicators of abuse comes from practitioners. Due to the idea being that dissociation and repression helps to protect a person from pain of trauma.

I definitely see where they're coming from because this is a very logical idea and response to trauma by the body.

The evidence for Recovered Memories comes largely from case studies and there are some early lab studies supporting this, but these lab studies didn't study trauma for ethical reasons so Sheehan (1997) suggests the cases were victims forget their trauma but offenders confirm it as a persuasive argument for repression.

Now that is interesting, because the clinical psychologists are saying that the offenders of abuse themselves support the Recovered Memory argument. This makes me question a couple of things, because my main question is are offenders a good source of information? It isn't the offenders that experience Recovered Memories, so these actually aren't that great of a source of information, in my opinion.

On the other hand, you have academics that have been a lot more dismissive of the research done by clinical practitioners because these ideas don't fit with their theoretical assumption of how memory is seen and doubters point out that in a dissociative state people are aware of what's missing from their memory, and this doesn't happen with recovered memories. Since in recovered memories people realise that they actually have memories, this doesn't happen in disassociated state.

Overall, Recovered Memory sceptics believe that there isn't sufficient evidence of dissociation and repression and how this is then applied to repeated experiences of rape.

<u>Elizabeth Loftus</u>

If you've been a reader of mine for a while then you know I have massive amounts of respect and interest in Loftus's work, because as a researcher, she has transformed the way we think of memory and her work is very useful in understanding the flaws of memory.

Therefore, one of Recovered Memories fiercest critics is Elizabeth Loftus (Loftus et al., 2008), because she argues that there's no evidence for repression and the example given to support repression are just "instances of old everyday forgetting" (page 178).

Which I have to admit I do sort of see where she's coming from.

In addition, Loftus pointed out that 50% of judges, 65% of police officers and 73% of jurors (Benton et al., 2006) believe that repression exists compared to only 22% of empirically oriented psychologists.

This is critical to understand because at the end

of the day, it doesn't matter what psychologists know as fact when it comes to legal systems. It matters from the people working in the Criminal Justice System believe in the exact way that psychologists know that psychological profiling is rubbish, but police officers and jurors think it is God's gift to the world.

Therefore, my point is cognitive researchers can argue as much as they want about the debate, but if it is ever settled then we have to make sure that other people know whether or not Repression is real. Granted I seriously doubt this will ever be the case and the debate will continue well after my lifetime.

Why Some Researchers Don't Choose A Side?

Personally, I have to admit that considering how opinionated, unprofessional and argumentative academics can be, I was rather amazed to learn that some researchers choose not to pick a side in this debate. For example, Memon and Young (1997) stressed the importance of exploring the possible mechanisms behind recovered memories. Also, they concluded that repression lacks supporting evidence that convincedly mimics the processes of repression as researchers describe it. As well as the so-called "grand" ideal of repression is dubious at best because of its questionable validity when repression means something other than gradually forgetting over time. Lastly, the researchers concluded that there's evidence that supports the idea that memories can be disassociated (as seen in Multiple Personality

Disorder), suppressed and inhibition.

Overall, there just isn't the firm research support for memory repression.

This is supported even more by flashbulb memories (Brown and Kulik, 1977). This is a special memory mechanism that creates vivid and highly detailed recordings of the event when the witnessing or receiving of the news of the event is unexpected and is emotionally arousing. This is problematic for Repression because rape and sexual abuse are exactly the sort of events when a flashbulb memory would be created instead of getting repressed.

Another theory that goes against Memory Repression is reconstructive theory. Which as I preluded to earlier it suggests that memories in the Long-term Memory isn't a passive process that stays the same as when the information is encoded. In fact, it could be an active recreation of the event every time we replay the event in our mind.

Additionally, the theory recognises that information that we encode during the event and after the event can; at least over time; merge together to form a new memory to the point where we can't tell them apart anymore.

Therefore, if we link this Reconstructive Theory into rape and sexual abuse, we know that children don't encode time, dates and things they don't understand so if an adult or teenager does include these then they were probably added into it later on.

In other words, adults could be putting the

memory into adult terms.

How Claims Of Recovered Memories Can Change?

Interestingly enough, claims of recovered memories can be made but later retracted too, and DeRiviera (1997) suggested the retraction of the claims can be down to a set of circumstances in how these memories were recovered in the first place. For instance, clients create a narrative that helps their life make sense by being put into a meaningful and constructive way, that is helped by a few suggestions from a therapist. As well as an authority figure (like an abuser) uses informational, emotional and behavioural techniques and thought control to control the victim's thoughts.

Another study is Ost et al. (2002) who studied retractors because by their very nature, evidence from retractors are suspect because of the person's flip-flopping. The study found that retractors claimed to be more confident about the retraction the more pressure they were under to recover the memories.

Leading us to question, why on Earth the majority of retractors said they were under no pressure to retract statements. Isn't that just a little of a contradiction?

On excellent example of this in real-life can be seen in Geraets, Raymaxkers and Merckelbach (2008) who looked at the story of Benjamin Wilomiski who claimed to spend his childhood in a Nazi concentration camp but only remembered this because of Dreams Interpretation therapy, but it turned out he spent his childhood in his foster parents' home in Switzerland. Yet Wilomiski was convinced his version was the truth.

Resulting in researchers exploring whether where people who claim to have recovered memories are actually just prone to false memory induction.

This can be seen in the Cognitive test of the Desse-Roediger-McDermott (DRM) paradigm (Desse, 1959) because this involves a list of words with one common feature that is a word not on the list. This is known as the critical lure. An example of Geraerts et al. (2008) is *awake, rest, bed, tired* and others.

In this case the critical lure was sleep resulting in some participants to believe them remembered seeing *sleep* on the list even though that's impossible.

And as unfortunate as it is people who recover child sexual abuse memories also tend to score a lot of errors on this test compared to a control group of people who had abused but never forgotten the events and another control group that didn't have any history of abuse. This study is further supported by Clancy, Schacter, McNally and Pitman, 2000.

What About Ecological validity?

I always like looking at ecological validity because it is critical that our results do show what happens in the real-world and just what happens in the lab. Yet poor ecological validity does create a lot of problems for researchers too, because a lot of the Repression "evidence" comes from case studies that show some people who claim to have recovered memories have spoken to others about it, but they don't remember these conversations so when they are magically recovered, they put it down as remembering for the first time since childhood.

Leading Geraerts et al. (2008) to do a lot of interviews and they found people have two types of recovered memories. Firstly, there is the spontaneous type. This is a recovered memory that is quicker to recover and almost takes the person by surprise. Secondly, there is the gradual type. This is a fairly slow type to recover and normally involves suggestive therapies like hypnosis.

Overall, these types were explained further with 4 groups and the researchers found the groups involved in memory recovery during suggestive therapy were particularly error prone. As well as the spontaneous recovery group was more capable of suppressing memories when asked to do so under lab conditions. Also, Gleaves and Smith (2004) reviewed literature and found support for both types.

On the whole, at the end of this chapter, I think it is fairly safe to say that this is an area of research that is massive and filled with answers and counterarguments no matter what side of the debate you fall on. This isn't going to get sorted out for ages and when it comes to False Allegations that is a shame.

But now, we need to focus on fake claims of child sexual abuse, because why on Earth would someone want to fake these horrific claims?

Let's find out.

FALSE CLAIMS OF SEXUAL ABUSE AND YOUNG CHILDREN

Whilst this might be one of the most heart-wrenching and difficult chapters so far in the book, because we need to investigate how evidence coming from children can lead to false allegations, I want to remind you that this is extremely important and this chapter does not go into any graphic details.

In addition, I absolutely have to stress that this chapter is flat out not saying that all evidence from children is unreliable. All claims must be taken extremely seriously.

Therefore, there is an issue about children giving evidence and how this evidence might be encouraged by an interviewer to claim things that never happened.

The interest into this research area really grew in 1980 after the McMartin School and other cases were children seemed to accuse teachers of kidnapping and taking them to a remote island for group sex and satanic torture. The end result of the cases were that charges against all the teachers were eventually dropped after reviewing the interviews and this review found that the interviewers made suggestions and other techniques that made the children end up giving poor evidence about things that never happened. One of these techniques was for the interviewer to suggest how good the memories of the children were so the children were more confident about these events that didn't happen (Garwen, Wood and Malpass, 2000).

These findings about interviewing leading to poor evidence from children is supported by other preschool children studies as well. Like Bruck et al., (1995) and Ceci et al., (1994).

Thankfully for us interested in psychology research, it isn't hard to study how fake accusations can be made by pre-schoolers. Since around a third of preschool children accept fictional events as real, with this remaining the same over multiple interviews. Resulting in little inconsistency, but researchers saying the fictional event was real increased beliefs.

Overall, this convincing children that events that didn't happen actually happened is called "False memory induction" and this very much depends on age.

Since children do accept fiction as real on occasion when it is elaborative and someone describes the emotions associated with it. Yet these results are only suggestive of extent in a real interview condition where young children mix up the truth or not.

This research lacks ecological validity, as well as other research limitations that include:

- Questioning went way beyond what's expected of social workers and police officers when interviewing a child suspected of possible sexual abuse.
- Age group isn't representative of the age of children involved in sexual abuse allegations as well as fake memory induction may not apply to older children.
- Findings might not apply to real-life situations.

As a result, as you can see from the limitations above, the massive problem with this literature is that it can all be boiled down into ecological validity issues. Meaning future research needs to make more of real interviewing transcripts. Yet I do truly understand the ethical, legal and other complicated issues this ecologically valid research would bring up.

How Can We Overcome Suggestive Interviewing?

As you can see from the sections above, suggestive interviewing can be awful when it comes to false allegations and searching for the truth about what actually happened to a child. Therefore, we do need to find ways to overcome these interviewing errors.

Leading us onto Poole and Lindsay (1998) because these researchers suggested that a child needs to know that the interviewee only wants them to report on real experiences, situations and they wanted children to know where they got their sources of information from. For example, did they witness it, did it happen to them or did someone else tell them about the abuse.

This means that the child needs a source monitoring ability.

As a result, this led the researchers to create Poole and Lindsay's Mr Science lab experiment and this involved real science lessons with children where the researchers sent them a storybook to the children containing the real lessons and some fictional ones involving fictional abuse before the researchers interviewed them.

The study found that leading questions in the interviewing increased the rates of fake reporting as well as this remained stable in a free recall test because researchers found that increasing the age range of the children from 3 to 8 did not cause a decline in false reporting.

In addition, the study found that 2/5 of the research sample mentioned that the false events were real, but some good news is that when the researchers challenged the children about the truth, this did lead to a decrease in older children, but not younger children.

Furthermore, these children that were severely challenged did continue to claim Mr Science did truly put something yucky in their mouths. Therefore, it is clear that even if a police officer challenges a child again and again and the child sticks to their story, it sadly doesn't always mean the story is true.

Also, these results have a fairly high stability because a follow-up study 2 months later revealed two-thirds of the children were still making fake claims.

Could Children Be Resistant To Leading Questions?

Although, we have to understand that just because children can be influenced by leading questions, it doesn't mean this is a universal rule of behaviour that will always, always happen no matter what. Since Leichtman and Ceci (1995) supports the argument that children are somewhat resistant to leading questions, as they were researching 3-6-year-olds about Sam Stone visiting their school, looking around and then leave. These 3 to 6-year-olds were interviewed 4 times about the visit and there were no suggestive techniques used so far and then the children were gently challenged with questions.

The results of the study showed that the researchers found high accuracy was produced amongst the children because only 10% of the sample said he did something to teddy or a book when he didn't and this was reduced to 5% when asked if he actually did it.

Then the researchers did the study again with another group of pre-schoolers when these children were exposed to repeated conversations about Sam's clumsiness and how he was prone to breaking things.

Then the pre-schoolers were interviewed and they were asked if he broke anything using a suggestive question.

The results showed that the leading question caused 72% of the research sample to report that Sam Stone did something to the book or teddy. Then when challenged this decreased to 44% when asked if they actually saw him do this and then this reduced to 21% of children maintaining their fake stories when gently challenged.

I think this is a very useful study because it shows that children can give reliable evidence when challenged and questioned. But even after challenging multiple times, 21% of children still maintained false allegations against Sam Stone and I won't lie the ecological validity of this study is somewhat questionable. Yet the point is still clear. Children can resist leading questions but not entirely.

Moreover, the older children in the study, 5 to 6 year-olds, were found to be less malleable than younger children as only 11% of this higher age group reported they saw it with less than 10% of this section of the sample maintaining their stories.

However, as annoying as this limitation of the research is, the real life issue about children falling for leading questions and maintaining stories about events that never happened is a lot more complex than this current research because sexual abuse cases are in the hands of professionals that must make decisions.

Leading us on nicely to our next section.

How Good Are Professionals At Detecting Fake Information?

In this next section, we're going to be focusing on how good and accurate professionals at are detecting fake information. This is a brilliant topic that I do enjoy and if this is a topic that really interests you and you want to see it in a larger, more boarder police context, then definitely check out Police Psychology.

The first study we'll look at comes from Horner, Guiyer and Kalter (1993) who gave workers in the mental health field plenty of case studies with parent interviews, child interviews and details on child-parent interactions and they got the workers to make a decision on whether abuse was happening or not. The results showed that regardless of whether the workers believed the abuse happened or not, they always recommended the children should see the father in a supervised setting.

And this is the thing that makes this topic really interesting, because there has to be a bias going on. Since these workers couldn't decide if abuse was happening and yet, they felt the need to protect the child from the father out of instinct (for lack of a better term). Now in a study this is okay but if this sort of bias played out in the real world then this could result in a child being ripped away from their innocent father.

This isn't an easy decision to make though

because child protection must always come first.

Moreover, clinical and research psychologists who specialise in interviewing children watched videos of children in the mousetrap experiment. The results showed the psychologists were no more able to tell the differences between real and fictional abuse better than at the chance level (Ceci et al., 1994).

Following on from this, Bruck and Ceci (1997) used the above research as well as other studies as evidence of the creation of suggestive interviews based on the interviewer's biases. Implying that the interviewer creates these suggestive techniques used in interviews as a result of their own biases.

These biases are seen as becoming involved in the interview process because if the child's statement supports what the interviewer thinks happened then the interviewer doesn't challenge the child even when they really should as a matter of good practice. As well as the interviewer bias shows up again when we consider how the interviewer doesn't touch on events or conversations that don't support what they believed happened.

The Concept of Suggestibility And False Allegations

Whilst this entire chapter has really focused on suggestibility in all but name, now we need to call it out and really focus on the concept of suggestibility, a concept that has a long history in psychology. This is a notion that a lot of people are familiar with in the Criminal Justice System and children protection since William (1904) discussed some people are predisposed to fall to suggestion as a person's suggestibility.

Before we get too far ahead, I have to admit that I always weary about concepts and theories that laypeople get too excited about, simply because it is always the wrong theories they get excited about. Like profiling that is rubbish in reality, their awful understanding of therapy and so on.

In addition, it's important that we separate suggestibility into its two different types. Firstly, there is passive suggestibility and this is a state of where a person is under the influence of suggestion. Secondly, you have active suggestibility and this is the activity of suggesting something to another

These can be totally unrelated, as well as people can make a suggestion that isn't responded to, and a suggestion that never happened can be responded to.

Therefore, just because someone does try to make a suggestion towards another person, a suggestion's influence cannot always be blamed for behaviour, because the influence might be smaller or different than we think.

For instance, Ceci and Bruck (1993) demonstrated that suggestibility refers to the extent of which all aspects of a child's memory are affected by psychological and social factors. Making it a mistake to limit suggestibility down to an interviewer's questions or interview style.

This mistake is summed up perfectly here Motzkau (2004) "suggestibility is itself suggestive," (page 7).

In addition, if we go back to what I was mentioning earlier about laypeople and people within the Criminal Justice System often getting the wrong end of the stick, it is the widespread knowledge of suggestibility that has a wide range of effects on the Criminal Justice System that goes far beyond our current research base.

Moreover, what I hate about all this is whenever psychological concepts leak into the public, the public have a very simplistic understanding of any concept leading them to overstate results of research (Motzkau, 2004). Like believing children are easy to fall to suggestions and are tricked by others into making false allegations.

When as we're seen from the different studies mentioned in the book, this isn't a clear-cut result and children aren't as suggestible as believed.

On the whole, everyone needs to take much, much greater care around the topic of the suggestibility of children. Due to children aren't always under any suggestive influence and research doesn't mean that younger children are more suggestible than older children or even adults. Even older children and adults can be suggestible.

There's even some evidence that older children and adults might be even suggestible on some topics but not others. Such as, Eisen et al. (1988) showed us that abused children were suggestible on mundane topics and younger children when compared to older children were more suggestible. But when it came to the critical topic of abuse, the young children were not so suggestible compared to mundane topics.

And this I think can be linked to flashbulb memories because when you have been abused and experience something awful then you will remember what you see.

Another problem with the research on suggestibility and the reliability of children is that there is little consistency in studies as to the percentage of children who fall for a suggestive question. (Poole and Lindsay, 2002). This is annoying for psychology researchers because it makes it impossible to know the true extent of suggestion's role in real-life cases.

How To Do Good Interviews?

After learning a lot about bad interviewing, we need to understand how can people do good interviewing when it comes to young children. The answer is that when good interviewing methods are used they can minimize false allegations rates, and might eliminate them entirely.

As a result, one way to improve interviewing is by using interviewing protocols developed for professionals. As seen in Hershkowitz, Lamb and Katz (2014) when they studied Israeli children sent for abuse investigating using the NICHD (National Institute of Child Health and Human Development) Investigate Interview Protocol. This is a research-based tool that focuses on increasing rapport and takes account of social, linguistic and cognitive factors that limit how informative the children's account of abuse will be. The researchers conducted the study using two versions of the protocol, a standard one and a revised one.

The results found that the Revised one resulted in even more rapport and more allegations being made. As well as 56% of children out of 400+ children made some sort of abuse allegation and all of them were supported with independent evidence. Suggesting the protocol results in more allegations than would be expected to be made without any false allegations.

That is definitely some good news that I want to end this chapter with because before we become interested in psychology, we are laypeople. I've heard all the stories about how children cannot be trusted when it comes to abuse and all that other rubbish. But if you take anything away from this chapter, let it be that when a child says something there is a good chance that they are telling the truth and they should never ever be dismissed just because of their age.

That realisation is simply critical when it comes to false allegations.

THE DIAGNOSTIC SIGNS OF ABUSE

Personally, I definitely think this is a really interesting chapter and topic when it comes to false allegations and child sexual abuse, because it seems that some researchers are seriously interested in finding out if there are a set of signs that can "prove" that a child has been abused.

I think this is interesting because if this does turn out to be the case then this would give social workers, police officers and other professionals working in the area of sexual abuse another powerful tool in their work. But personally, I think this sounds like a fantasy because as us psychology people know, things are very, very rarely able to prove something especially when it comes down to simply finding some behavioural signs.

If you're aware of the current problems with the mental health classification and diagnosis models then you'll be aware of what I mean.

Anyway, as you can imagine when it comes to

child sexual abuse, clinicians, psychologists and other professionals focus on a limited range of people. For example, they only focus on the severely abused people, because this is the group of abused people that are the clearest to see.

Therefore, these professionals have their knowledge developed as a result of these limited people in this limited group. This means that the psychologists and other professionals can theorise that if abused people in this group have a common symptom, like bedwetting during childhood, then these symptoms could be applied to other people.

The first problem this creates is an illusory correlation bias where people think that two or more variables are linked when they actually aren't since professionals could believe bedwetting is always a sign of abuse when it actually isn't.

To explore this, Bradley and Wood (1996) showed that nearly 75% of children that they studied had already revealed their abuse to someone before they came to the attention of the police or child protection services. As well as only 6% of the children in the study denied their abuse, and having a child recant their statement was rare at 4%. This is important because it reinforces what I mentioned in the last chapter about if a child does deny an abuse allegation then they probably aren't lying.

In addition, Berliner and Conte (1993) argued for professionals to use caution when looking at studies that find a higher prevalence of mental conditions in sexually abused children compared to non-abused children. This is because the argument makes no sense. Since it is only a select few, if any, factors of any mental health conditions that are uniquely found in abused children, and even when studies do find these factors, most of this data comes from self-reported data from children and parents, with parent showing large differences between the two groups.

The problem with this is that self-reported data just isn't as empirical, bullet-proof or reliable compared to other behavioural measurements. Due to self-reported data is all subjective, it's about what someone feels and if you're familiar with developmental psychology. Then this is where issues like egocentrism, peer pressure and more come into play.

Leading us onto the next concept in this chapter.

<u>Why Is Diagnosticity A Key Concept?</u>

When it comes to diagnostic symptoms, these are real for the most part and different mental health conditions do have unique symptoms that psychologists can use to identify them. Or these symptoms appear in different clusters so they all point towards a different condition.

For example, whilst both depression and bipolar disorder involve low moods, only bipolar disorder has manic episodes. Therefore, these can be really useful to psychologists because they can give them a place to start when it comes to intervention options for clients.

However, there are those working in the areas of child sexual abuse that want to look at diagnostic symptoms for children that look at the extent to which a child's behaviour and attitude indicated they were abused.

A rather early study into this argument comes from Howitt (1992) who detailed out a range of factors that are suggested indicators of abuse. For example, how a child response to their anus being touched by a doctor is one suggestive indicator. (Hanks, Hobbs and Wynne, 1988).

Now as you can imagine, the idea of this approach might be flawed but there are surprisingly enough some encouraging research findings.

For instance, Slusser (1995) conducted a review and they used an extremely high number of studies (6 whole studies) and the researcher concluded that overt sexual behaviour that is inappropriate for children of that age is an indication of abuse.

Despite the fact that it has to be noted that sometimes child sexual activity as a baseline is high.

Furthermore, Gordon, Schroeder and Abrams (1990a, b) investigated this area in a different way by getting parental reports on 2–7-year-old children. The researchers found that 50% of these really young children had masturbated, 30% of the children had been involved in exploratory sex-play, as well as 29% of the family claimed that their children had been exposed to sexually explicit material.

Now another problem with these results is social

desirability bias coming from two different places. Firstly, all these numbers could be lower the reality of what happens, because come on, if you know you're 5-year-old child is doing something related to sex play then by God are you not going to tell anyone. You really aren't and you certainly aren't going to tell a researcher that you, as a layperson, might be concerned about would report you to child services or something. Especially as it never stops amazing me how much people don't know about real research and ethics.

Equally, the social desirability bias can work the other way. Since if a very nice researcher has come to you wanting to know some information, there is a chance that the parents just told the researcher what they wanted to hear. It is possible.

Furthermore, if we take a break for a moment and focus on offenders, we cannot get reliable indicators from them either. Since Munchausen's syndrome by proxy conditions are a range of conditions where an offender fakes abuse symptoms and hurts a child to receive repeated medical attention (Plassan, 1994). As well as these symptoms by the offenders are often diametrically opposite (Howitt, 1992) because offenders both confess to and deny the crime and they are often both uncaring and overly concerned about the child's health.

What Makes An Indicator Valuable?

Let's say for the sake of argument that researchers have managed to find a very good indicator that confirms that childhood sexual abuse did occur. I have to admit that these indicators are only valuable to professionals if they meet certain conditions.

For example, an indicator of abuse cannot be similar between abused and non-abused children. As well as the frequency of the indicator of abuse has to be higher in abused children or rare or non-existent in non-abused children.

However, the problem is that very often researchers simply don't know the relative frequency in the overall population, and if the indicator of abuse is equal between the populations then it's useless to professionals.

In addition, Finlayson and Koocher (1991) found that children psychologists vary massively in their interpretation of suggestive indicators. Also, Slusser (1995) suggests that certain indicators with high base rates anyway may have different causes that have absolutely nothing to do with abuse. Bedwetting is a great example of this because it can be caused by abuse but it can be caused by smaller bladder capacity, stress, alcohol intoxication, a urinary track infection amongst other causes.

Overall, all these indicators have little value at this point in time.

Of course, research is the only way to know if indicators are reliable and if there's a difference between abused and non-abused people. Due to Friedrich et al. (1992) conducted an extensive investigation into parental reports of child sexual behaviour. The researchers found that there were certain behaviours that had similar rates between groups so these are truly useless indicators.

However, when it comes to some factors like masturbation, the story can get interesting. Since another undated Friedrich study found that abused 2-5-year-old females are more likely to masturbate than other people. For the sake of clarity masturbation happened at 28% for the abused group and only 16% the non-abused group).

Nonetheless, this does suggest that there is a clear association but things aren't so simple because if we take a class of 30 children and we don't know the firm average of abuse, and wider range of age group factors and survey results. It's unreasonable to suppose only or even 10% of the class was abused, 90% have never been or something that simple. All based off the masturbation indicator.

As a result, there should be a clear requirement of any indicator approach to be more demanding than it first appears (Wood, 1996) because this isn't easy.

This could mean that when a list of indicators are reproduced with the research to support it, finding indicators that are 3 times more likely to happen in abused children could be a weak argument that abuse has happened or finding indicators that are 14 times more likely to happen in abused children might be a moderate or stronger argument for abuse.

Although, this is still far from perfect proof of

abuse (Poole and Lindsay, 1998) because let's face it, finding indicators that are 14 times higher in any clinical people is next to impossible. This is why when it comes to mental health we have to add in the factor about *the difficulty has to cause clinically significant levels of distress and impairment in core areas of functioning.* Since everyone gets a low mood but not everyone gets to such a low mood that they feel like it is impossible to get out of bed in the mornings.

On the whole, the interpretation of ratios like this could be hard for practitioners as well as psychologists to apply and appreciate. I will admit that I am finding this approach very hard to appreciate in case my tone isn't clear.

As well as Friedrich et al. (1992) found children trying to achieve an intimation of intercourse is 14 times more likely in abused children compared to only 1% of non-abusers.

Although, this is a tricky one because caution needs to be added here as a child's sexual activity could be heightened by the sexual abuse investigation itself.

In conclusion of this chapter, it does seem sensible for us to look for 2 indicators but this idea does little in reality because of the weak predictive strength of indicators and these different indicators tend to co-occur anyway so this does very little to improve diagonality overall.

IN WHAT WAYS ARE GENUINE ALLEGATIONS DIFFERENT FROM FALSE ALLEGATIONS?

In the final chapter of the book, we need to answer a simple question that the entire book has been leading up to. Since we've spent the past six chapters looking at a whole range of factors behind false allegations, so how can you tell the difference between a real one and a false allegation?

To put it very, very simply, you can't. There is no easy way of telling the difference but there are certain signs a person might be able to look for to have a feeling or indication about whether it's true or not.

Since Marshall and Alison (2006) termed *Structured Behavioural Analysis* to examine the behavioural characteristics of real and fake rape allegations. They got real allegations statements from the police and fake ones were women weren't abused but tried to convince the police otherwise.

Following this the researchers looked at 37

indicators in these reports. For example, whether kissing was involved, cunnilingus involved, whether the offender made sexual comments, if the victim was bound, if there was anal penetration and many more.

Interestingly enough, there were differences between the two types of reports. Since in the real reports, the researchers were able to produce more behaviourally coherent reports than the fictional ones.

Also, the real accounts contained more pseudo-intimate details, like the offenders offering the details about themselves to the victim and victim receiving compliments. As well as compared to the real reports, fake ones contained less normal sexual activity. Like cunnilingus, fellatio and anal penetration.

Finally, the fictional reports were more likely to contain violent acts against the victim.

Overall, the indication from this method of analysis did find that the analysis was better at finding out true accounts compared to fake ones.

So does this suggest that it is easier to tell fake accounts compared to real ones?

Peace, Porter and Almon (2012) conducted a very in-depth study literally providing students with everything they needed to make a correct decision on the 4 true and 4 fake allegations and students only got 45% cases right.

Making it better to just flip a coin.

This happened because the students tended to judge sexual assault narratives as more truthful, suggesting a bias in this part of the process. Also, students were more likely to judge narratives correctly but still at an equal chance level.

Overall, researchers concluded that a person's emotionality leads to poor accuracy outcomes at truth-judging tasks like this one.

This isn't great when it comes to dealing with such horrific crimes and having a sex offender out on the loose. This is why like I mentioned back at the beginning of the book, a proper police investigation is flat out critical, before it is just dismissed as Unfounded or No Crime.

CONCLUSION

At the end of this book, I have to admit that we have covered a hell of a lot of different topics. We have looked at why the entire area of false allegation isn't really a psychological area because it is more of a legal question. Then we started to realise that false allegations are behaviours of people who have motivations, thinking and memory biases and a lot of other psychological factors play a role in false allegations.

We explored a lot of them.

In addition, whilst we covered false allegations and child sexual abuse in a lot of depth, I made sure that we didn't cover anything graphic or any case studies that might offend people too much. Since I know this is an extremely heart-breaking and concerning for people especially if you have children or you know young children yourselves. For example, I have two nieces and a nephew at the time of writing (I might have more in the future) and I would absolutely be furious if anything happened to them.

Yet this is another reason why forensic psychology as well as all other fields of psychology are so critical. All these fields help us to understand, keep learning and keep pushing our knowledge base further so we can understand why the hell people commit such awful behaviours.

Due to the massive problem with false allegations is that a single one can cast doubt on thousands of real cases of child abuse. Meaning that it is very possible that innocent children, innocent women and innocent men that are being abused will simply not be believed because of a single false allegation.

This is why I said in the introduction of the book that I wrote this book not to encourage you to disbelieve allegations of rape, abuse and sexual assault. That isn't what this book has found and this entire book has been dedicated to all the survivors, victims and sadly future victims of these awful crimes. Because I want them to know that there is great research that shows us that the majority of people when they develop that amazing courage to come forward, they aren't lying, probably.

And it is only the minority that lie about these most horrific crimes.

Also, going back to the research angle for a moment, researchers might not know or have any good indicators of abuse. But to be honest, given the sheer amount of research this book has looked at that suggests that victims are the best judges of the crime that happened against them. I don't think this is needed.

I know we have to develop better ways to find evidence of rape, sexual assault and abuse so convictions can increase. Since rape convictions are extremely low and that is never good.

But that is also where psychology comes in and other researchers. It is only through research that these problems will get solved, so please dear reader if you are of the research persuasion then please think about researching this area. It will be hard but it is so important.

And if you're not interested in research (I'm definitely not) then if you take any single thing away from this book, please let it be that just because someone makes an allegation of rape, abuse or sexual assault. It flat out doesn't mean they are lying.

Not every allegation is a false allegation. Just remember that and maybe someone can get justice in the end.

REFERENCES

Berliner, L., & Conte, J. R. (1993). Sexual abuse evaluations: Conceptual and empirical obstacles. *Child Abuse & Neglect, 17*(1), 111-125.

Bradley, A. R., & Wood, J. M. (1996). How do children tell? The disclosure process in child sexual abuse. *Child abuse & neglect, 20*(9), 881-891.

Brown, J., Shell, Y. & Cole, T. (2015). Forensic Psychology: Theory, research, policy and practice. 1st edition

Bruck, M., & Ceci, S. J. (1997). The suggestibility of young children. *Current Directions in Psychological Science, 6*(3), 75-79.

Bruck, M., Ceci, S. J., Francoeur, E., & Barr, R. (1995). "I hardly cried when I got my shot!" Influencing children's reports about a visit to their pediatrician. *Child Development, 66*(1), 193-208.

Ceci, S. J., Loftus, E. F., Leichtman, M. D., & Bruck, M. (1994). The possible role of source misattributions in the creation of false beliefs among preschoolers. *International Journal of Clinical and experimental hypnosis, 42*(4), 304-320.

Gordon, B. N., Schroeder, C. S., & Abrams, J. M. (1990). Age and social-class differences in children's knowledge of sexuality. *Journal of Clinical Child Psychology, 19*(1), 33-43.

Hanks, H., Hobbs, C., & Wynne, J. (1988). Early signs and recognition of sexual abuse in the preschool child. *Early prediction and prevention of child abuse*, 139-160.

Hershkowitz, I., Lamb, M. E., & Katz, C. (2014). Allegation rates in forensic child abuse investigations: Comparing the revised and standard NICHD protocols. *Psychology, Public Policy, and Law, 20*(3), 336.

Horner, T. M., Guyer, M. J., & Kalter, N. M. (1993). The biases of child sexual abuse experts: believing is seeing. *The Bulletin of the American Academy of Psychiatry and the Law, 21*(3), 281-292.

Howitt, D. (2018). Introduction to forensic and criminal psychology. Essex, UK: Pearson. 6th edition.

Leichtman, M. D., & Ceci, S. J. (1995). The effects of stereotypes and suggestions on preschoolers' reports. *Developmental Psychology, 31*(4), 568.

Lindsay, D. S., & Poole, D. A. (1998). The Poole et al.(1995) surveys of therapists: Misinterpretations by both sides of the recovered memories controversy. *The Journal of Psychiatry & Law, 26*(3), 383-399.

Motzkau, J. F. (2006). *Cross-examining suggestibility:*

Memory, childhood, expertise (Doctoral dissertation, Loughborough University).

Motzkau, J. F. (2009). Exploring the transdisciplinary trajectory of suggestibility. *Subjectivity*, *27*, 172-194.

Poole, D. A., & Lindsay, D. S. (1998). Assessing the accuracy of young children's reports: Lessons from the investigation of child sexual abuse. *Applied and Preventive Psychology*, *7*(1), 1-26.

Poole, D. A., & Lindsay, D. S. (2002). Reducing child witnesses' false reports of misinformation from parents. *Journal of Experimental Child Psychology*, *81*(2), 117-140.

Wood, J. & Gannon, T.A. (2009). Public opinion and criminal justice. Devon, UK: Willan Publishing

GET YOUR EXCLUSIVE FREE 8 BOOK PSYCHOLOGY BOXSET AND YOUR EMAIL PSYCHOLOGY COURSE HERE!

https://www.subscribepage.com/psychologyboxset

CHECK OUT THE PSYCHOLOGY WORLD PODCAST FOR MORE PSYCHOLOGY INFORMATION! AVAILABLE ON ALL MAJOR PODCAST APPS.

About the author:

Connor Whiteley is the author of over 60 books in the sci-fi fantasy, nonfiction psychology and books for writer's genre and he is a Human Branding Speaker and Consultant.

He is a passionate warhammer 40,000 reader, psychology student and author.

Who narrates his own audiobooks and he hosts The Psychology World Podcast.

All whilst studying Psychology at the University of Kent, England.

Also, he was a former Explorer Scout where he gave a speech to the Maltese President in August 2018 and he attended Prince Charles' 70th Birthday Party at Buckingham Palace in May 2018.

Plus, he is a self-confessed coffee lover!

THE FORENSIC PSYCHOLOGY OF FALSE ALLEGATIONS

All books in 'An Introductory Series':
Careers In Psychology
Psychology of Suicide
Dementia Psychology
Clinical Psychology Reflections Volume 4
Forensic Psychology of Terrorism And Hostage-Taking
Forensic Psychology of False Allegations
Year In Psychology
CBT For Anxiety
CBT For Depression
Applied Psychology
BIOLOGICAL PSYCHOLOGY 3RD EDITION
COGNITIVE PSYCHOLOGY THIRD EDITION
SOCIAL PSYCHOLOGY- 3RD EDITION
ABNORMAL PSYCHOLOGY 3RD EDITION
PSYCHOLOGY OF RELATIONSHIPS- 3RD EDITION
DEVELOPMENTAL PSYCHOLOGY 3RD EDITION
HEALTH PSYCHOLOGY
RESEARCH IN PSYCHOLOGY
A GUIDE TO MENTAL HEALTH AND TREATMENT AROUND THE WORLD-

CONNOR WHITELEY

A GLOBAL LOOK AT DEPRESSION
FORENSIC PSYCHOLOGY
THE FORENSIC PSYCHOLOGY OF THEFT, BURGLARY AND OTHER CRIMES AGAINST PROPERTY
CRIMINAL PROFILING: A FORENSIC PSYCHOLOGY GUIDE TO FBI PROFILING AND GEOGRAPHICAL AND STATISTICAL PROFILING.
CLINICAL PSYCHOLOGY
FORMULATION IN PSYCHOTHERAPY
PERSONALITY PSYCHOLOGY AND INDIVIDUAL DIFFERENCES
CLINICAL PSYCHOLOGY REFLECTIONS VOLUME 1
CLINICAL PSYCHOLOGY REFLECTIONS VOLUME 2
Clinical Psychology Reflections Volume 3
CULT PSYCHOLOGY
Police Psychology

A Psychology Student's Guide To University
How Does University Work?
A Student's Guide To University And Learning
University Mental Health and Mindset

THE FORENSIC PSYCHOLOGY OF FALSE ALLEGATIONS

<u>Other books by Connor Whiteley:</u>
<u>Bettie English Private Eye Series</u>
A Very Private Woman
The Russian Case
A Very Urgent Matter
A Case Most Personal
Trains, Scots and Private Eyes
The Federation Protects
Cops, Robbers and Private Eyes
Just Ask Bettie English
An Inheritance To Die For
The Death of Graham Adams
Bearing Witness
The Twelve
The Wrong Body
The Assassination Of Bettie English

<u>Lord of War Origin Trilogy:</u>
Not Scared Of The Dark
Madness
Burn Them All

<u>The Fireheart Fantasy Series</u>
Heart of Fire
Heart of Lies
Heart of Prophecy
Heart of Bones

Heart of Fate

<u>City of Assassins (Urban Fantasy)</u>
City of Death
City of Marytrs
City of Pleasure
City of Power

<u>Agents of The Emperor</u>
Return of The Ancient Ones
Vigilance
Angels of Fire
Kingmaker
The Eight
The Lost Generation
Hunt
Emperor's Council
Speaker of Treachery
Birth Of The Empire
Terraforma

<u>The Rising Augusta Fantasy Adventure Series</u>
Rise To Power
Rising Walls
Rising Force
Rising Realm

THE FORENSIC PSYCHOLOGY OF FALSE ALLEGATIONS

<u>Lord Of War Trilogy (Agents of The Emperor)</u>
Not Scared Of The Dark
Madness
Burn It All Down

<u>Gay Romance Novellas</u>
Breaking, Nursing, Repairing A Broken Heart
Jacob And Daniel
Fallen For A Lie
Spying And Weddings

<u>Miscellaneous:</u>
RETURN
FREEDOM
SALVATION
Reflection of Mount Flame
The Masked One
The Great Deer
English Independence

OTHER SHORT STORIES BY CONNOR WHITELEY

<u>Mystery Short Story Collections</u>
Criminally Good Stories Volume 1: 20 Detective Mystery Short Stories
Criminally Good Stories Volume 2: 20 Private Investigator Short Stories
Criminally Good Stories Volume 3: 20 Crime Fiction Short Stories
Criminally Good Stories Volume 4: 20 Science Fiction and Fantasy Mystery Short Stories
Criminally Good Stories Volume 5: 20 Romantic Suspense Short Stories

<u>Mystery Short Stories:</u>
Protecting The Woman She Hated
Finding A Royal Friend
Our Woman In Paris
Corrupt Driving
A Prime Assassination
Jubilee Thief
Jubilee, Terror, Celebrations
Negative Jubilation
Ghostly Jubilation
Killing For Womenkind
A Snowy Death

THE FORENSIC PSYCHOLOGY OF FALSE ALLEGATIONS

Miracle Of Death
A Spy In Rome
The 12:30 To St Pancreas
A Country In Trouble
A Smokey Way To Go
A Spicy Way To GO
A Marketing Way To Go
A Missing Way To Go
A Showering Way To Go
Poison In The Candy Cane
Kendra Detective Mystery Collection Volume 1
Kendra Detective Mystery Collection Volume 2
Mystery Short Story Collection Volume 1
Mystery Short Story Collection Volume 2
Criminal Performance
Candy Detectives
Key To Birth In The Past

<u>Science Fiction Short Stories:</u>
Their Brave New World
Gummy Bear Detective
The Candy Detective
What Candies Fear
The Blurred Image
Shattered Legions

The First Rememberer
Life of A Rememberer
System of Wonder
Lifesaver
Remarkable Way She Died
The Interrogation of Annabella Stormic
Blade of The Emperor
Arbiter's Truth
Computation of Battle
Old One's Wrath
Puppets and Masters
Ship of Plague
Interrogation
Edge of Failure

<u>Fantasy Short Stories:</u>
City of Snow
City of Light
City of Vengeance
Dragons, Goats and Kingdom
Smog The Pathetic Dragon
Don't Go In The Shed
The Tomato Saver
The Remarkable Way She Died
Dragon Coins
Dragon Tea
Dragon Rider

www.ingramcontent.com/pod-product-compliance
Lightning Source LLC
LaVergne TN
LVHW012125070526
838202LV00056B/5865